All About Strange Beasts of the Past

allabout
books

All About
Strange Beasts
of the Past

By Roy Chapman Andrews
Former Director, American Museum of Natural History

Illustrated by Matthew Kalmenoff

RANDOM HOUSE
NEW YORK

This book

is for my delightful granddaughter

SARA ELIZABETH ANDREWS

Contents

Saber-toothed tiger

1.

Tragedy of the Tar Pits

Imagine time turned back almost a million years. That was the beginning of the Ice Age in America. Great fields of ice covered much of the northern part of the continent.

The country near what is now the city of Los Angeles, California, looked much as it does today. In the wide valley at Rancho La Brea, clumps of trees and bushes were scattered through tall grass.

To the east, the silver thread of a river could just be seen. In the foreground lay several strange-looking pools.

All About Strange Beasts of the Past

Each was surrounded by a bare black patch of ground on which nothing could grow. The pools were half-liquid asphalt, or tar. Through them at intervals broke bubbles of oil and evil-smelling gas. After a rain the surface was probably covered with a few inches of water. It was not good water, but it was drinkable. During dry weather a film of wind-blown dust made the tar look like solid ground. The pools, the valley and distant mountains, now called the Coast Range, shimmered in the hot sun of a summer's day.

A saber-toothed "tiger" which had just aroused from sleep looked over the valley from the summit of a shaded hill. He was a powerful beast, the most dreaded killer of the country. He had a short tail and massive front limbs. From either side of his upper jaw, nine-inch canine teeth projected downward. They were curved like sabers, sharp and pointed. No animal could stand against him. He wasn't really a tiger but he looked so much like one that tiger is what he is usually called.

The saber-toothed tiger was king of the country. All of it belonged to him by right of strength, ferocity and his terrible teeth. He stretched like a giant house cat and yawned. The lower jaw dropped, lying almost flat

The skull of the saber-tooth shows how the jaw dropped to open the mouth widely.

against his neck. Thus, his mouth could be opened widely. It gave him free use of his teeth as slashing knives or plunging daggers. Those teeth could cut through skin, flesh, and even bone.

The saber-tooth was a little hungry, but the sun beat down with blazing heat. Food in plenty roamed in front of him. He had only to select. But the day was hot, and he didn't want to exert himself. A herd of magnificent imperial mammoths lumbered along the skyline. They were forerunners of our living elephants, but larger.

Their great ivory tusks, curving inward, turned back the sun's rays like bars of polished steel.

But mammoths were not favorites of the saber-toothed tiger. They were too big, their skins too thick, their strength too great. At any time they would give a tough fight. Only when the great tiger could find a baby mammoth was it worth the trouble.

At one side, a group of camels browsed through the bushes and small trees. They were big animals, larger than camels of today. Their hair was thick, and they had

The early camel had no hump and was larger than today.

no humps of tissue and fat on their backs.

The saber-tooth looked at them with distaste. It would require effort to do a proper stalk and more effort to make the kill. He wasn't hungry enough. It was a lazy day. A little more sleep would be very good. He stretched luxuriously on the rock. His eyes closed, and his chin rested on his forepaws.

Half an hour later he waked suddenly. Some strange instinct brought him to his feet. In the valley below, his eye caught movement. Two huge, shaggy, golden-brown animals were pushing through the brush near a dry creek bed.

Instantly the tiger's body stiffened. His yellow eyes blazed. This was his favorite prey—the big, clumsy, slow-moving ground sloths. They were distant cousins of the small sloths, living today in South America, that hang on the underside of tree branches with hooked claws.

These ground sloths were larger than a grizzly bear. All through their skins were little pieces of bone. It gave them a kind of armor. Also, the hair was very thick and long. And they had great curved claws.

The sloths waddled about, sure that they were safe. They were safe enough from wolves and even lions, but not from the saber-tooth. He could cut through that tough skin with blows of his dagger teeth and rip open the jugular vein. He must be careful to avoid their claws, but that wasn't difficult. The ground sloths were too slow and stupid to worry him, and their flesh was very good.

The beasts were working their way toward the black pools. They were thirsty, and water from the previous night's rain glistened in the sun. They crossed the bare, black margin around the largest pool and splashed in to drink. For a few moments nothing happened. Then slowly the bottom began to yield. Their feet sank into gummy tar. Struggling in fright, they tried desperately to pull themselves out. But their hind legs only went deeper and deeper into the black ooze. Escape was impossible.

The saber-toothed tiger had left his hillock and crept silently through the brush. Belly down, chin almost touching the grass, his body seemed to flow across the ground. It was like the smooth movement of a snake. With eyes blazing, he watched the great beasts struggling in the pool. The time had come. In one bound, he flashed across the bare margin and leaped on the back of the

A great imperial mammoth was trapped in the tar pits of
La Brea.

nearest sloth. With a desperate wrench the animal threw him off. He rolled over in the asphalt. Snarling, the saber-tooth turned to strike at the golden-brown neck beside him. But he couldn't raise his feet. The sticky tar held them in a clutch of death. For the first time in his life, terror gripped his heart. Forgetting the sloths, he tried to drag himself out. But it was too late. He was sucked down slowly into the black depths of the asphalt pool.

From the bare branches of a tree, half a dozen great black vultures watched the tragedy being enacted below them. Huge birds they were, with naked red heads, enormous beaks, and ten-foot wings. These vultures were close relatives of the California condor that lives today. Like all vultures, they fed on dead flesh or helpless animals. They didn't kill for themselves as eagles and hawks do but waited until an animal died or had been caught.

While the sloths were still struggling in the clinging asphalt, the vultures circled over the trapped animals. One plopped down upon the surface of the pool. Then another and another. With hoarse croaks they surrounded the exhausted beasts. In a moment their great beaks would tear out chunks of living flesh. But as each bird tried to move, the sticky tar gripped its feet. Like insects on a sheet of flypaper, their wings and feathers were caught and held. Soon the scavengers of the plains were only black balls of tar. Long before the sun dropped behind the mountains, all trace of birds and beasts had disappeared. The pools glistened like silver. The traps were baited for new victims.

The story you have just read is true. It is imaginative only in details. We know it is true because of the fossil bones buried in the asphalt. Also because we can see the same tar traps operating today. The pits are not so large as they were a million years ago.

One morning I stood on the edge of one of the La Brea pools. A rabbit and a heron were struggling in the black ooze. A hawk circled overhead, coming lower and lower. I watched it dive for the rabbit. It sank its claws in the animal's body and tried to lift it out. In two minutes the bird itself was caught. Such has been the fate of many animals and birds through the years. Often cattle, horses and dogs have been caught in the asphalt. Some were dragged out with ropes. Others, not seen in time, died miserably. By this time the pits have been shut off so that wandering animals cannot be trapped by the deadly tar.

Originally the pools were formed by oil that oozed up from the earth in springs. Around the springs the tar remains soft. Elsewhere it hardens into a solid mass mixed with earth and wind-blown dust. In the Ice Age, the oil springs were more active than now.

When men began to take asphalt out of the La Brea pits to make roads, they discovered thousands of bones buried in the tar. For a time, little was done about it. Then scientists at the University of California began to study the strange bones. Thousands of skulls and tens of thousands of other bones have been dug out. The bones are filled with asphalt, but they have changed very little. Of course, nothing remains of the flesh, skin, horns and hoofs. The bones are jumbled up in a crowded mass so that the skeletons are never together.

The La Brea tar pits are famous as the richest fossil deposit ever discovered anywhere in the world. Nowhere else are the remains of so many different kinds of extinct animals found in one place. Nowhere else are the bones so well preserved. Nowhere else are they so easy to dig out and study.

As scientists have examined the La Brea fossils, they

have identified more than fifty different kinds of birds. They have found at least that many kinds of mammals, too. There are remains of elephants, camels and sloths; of deer, bison, horses and wild pigs. Three thousand skulls of the "grim wolf" and two thousand skulls of the saber-toothed tigers have been recovered. Also there are fossil bones of bears and lions and dozens of other beasts. Most of these creatures have been extinct for

Bison

Grim wolf

The bison and grim wolf were beasts of the Ice Age.

thousands and thousands of years.

Most of the bones are those of flesh-eating mammals, birds of prey and wading birds. The story of the saber-toothed tiger and the sloths and vultures gives the reason. The larger animals, caught in the asphalt, were bait for the trap. They lured flesh-eaters into the treacherous tar. Day after day this has gone on for a million years.

The remains of ducks, geese and herons are numerous. Perhaps they were attracted by the sheets of shimmering water on the tar and thought these were pleasant pools in which to swim.

The La Brea tar pits give a wonderful representation of the mammals that lived in southern California during the Ice Age. It is a whole chapter in the past life on this earth, written in black asphalt tar.

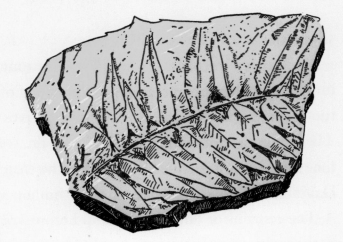

2.
Reading the Fossil Record

The word "fossil" comes from the Latin word *fossilis*, which means "dug up." Therefore, a fossil must have been buried at some time. It is the remains of a plant or animal that once lived upon the earth or in the water. Usually fossils are bones, but they can be rock impressions of plant or insects or shells or even footprints. Some fossils are millions of years old. Others may be only a few thousand years old.

Because of their great age fossils help us understand the story of past life. Some of them give us information about the world before man came upon the earth and made written records. From this information we can understand the present and predict some things about the future.

If a bone is not buried, it will be destroyed sooner or later. It may be destroyed by weather; for sun, rain, frost, snow and wind soon make powder out of bones. Also flesh-eating birds and animals, such as dogs, wolves, cats, hyenas, eagles and vultures, tear the carcass apart and carry off the bones. Even if there were no flesh eaters, little animals like rats and mice would gnaw the bones and destroy them. So a bone has little chance of surviving unless it is covered quickly by some sort of sediment.

Almost all fossils are found in what we call sedimentary rocks. The commonest kinds of sedimentary rocks are shales, which are hardened mud or clay, and sandstones, which are hardened sand. Limestone, another sedimentary rock, may be formed by lime dissolved in water or from the limy parts of animals or plants.

On dry land there is little chance for a bone to become a fossil. It might be covered quickly by blown sediment in a sand or dust storm, but that doesn't often happen.

The most usual way is for an animal to sink in quicksand, bogs or mud holes. That is what happened in the tar pits of Rancho La Brea.

Very often animals die on the banks of a stream or lake. A rainstorm or flood washes their bodies into the water. If there is no current, they may sink quietly into the mud. More probably, the carcass will drift downstream until it comes to rest in a backwater or eddy. There it drops to the bottom, the flesh slips away, and the bones lie naked. Then fine mud settles over the bones like dew on grass.

If a river carrying much sediment in its current pours into the backwater, the bones will be covered quickly. But sometimes months or years will pass before they are

Frequently animal bones will come to rest in a backwater or eddy of a lake or stream where they will be fossilized.

covered. Occasionally a skeleton is broken up by swift water, and all the bones are separated. They may be scattered far and wide over a large area. As they are rolled over and over on the bottom, only the hardest parts like the teeth and big bones remain.

Every bone is composed of hard and soft matter. When an animal dies, the soft matter usually decays, and the hard matter crumbles to dust. But if the bone is covered, a very slow change takes place. The soft matter disappears, leaving cavities and canals. These are filled by whatever mineral is in the earth where they are buried. If it is limestone, the bone cavities fill up with limestone and thus turn the bone to a fossil. Or it may be sandstone or even iron that transforms the original bones to fossil bones. I once found a dinosaur skeleton that had become iron. In that case the skeleton had been in water containing a great deal of iron. The iron had completely replaced the animal matter in the bones. In the La Brea tar pits the bone cavities were filled with tar or asphalt.

In the case of fossilized wood, the change is greater than in bone. The original vegetable matter is replaced by mineral substances. But even though the change is complete, the cellular form of the wood can still be seen under the microscope. In Arizona there is a place called the Petrified Forest. Here hundreds of fossilized trees lie on the ground. They have the shape of the original trees, but are now turned to stone.

Frequently we find stones that show the natural mold of a hard body, such as a sea shell. After the original shell was enclosed in mud or sand, it dissolved. Then the space was filled up with lime or silica which hardened into a fossil shaped like the original shell.

Fossil leaves are really imprints in stone. Suppose a leaf falls on the still surface of a pond and slowly sinks to the bottom where mud covers it. The vegetable matter rots away leaving a perfect impression of the leaf. Then

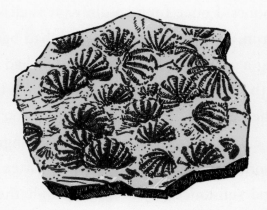

Sometimes the natural molds of sea shells are left in rock.

the minerals of the water fill the space made by the hard fibers of the leaf. These minerals turn to stone and we have a fossil imprint of the leaf. So it happens with plants of many kinds and also with insects. Their soft little bodies are cast in extremely fine mud which turns to stone. But the actual insect has disappeared.

By studying fossilized wood, plants, insects and animals, a scientist can tell about the climate millions of years ago. That is because the kinds of animals of a region indicate whether the country was plains or forest, and if there was much water, as in lakes or rivers. If the fossilized wood is that of conifers, such as pines or spruce, he can be sure that the climate was cold or temperate. If palms are found, he knows it must have been warm or tropical. So, with evidence from fossilized plants, animals, trees, and insects, the scientist can give a good picture of what the world was like at that time and place.

Fossils were once living things just as much as you and I are now, or as are your dog or cat and the plants around you. What makes one really understand this fact, is a fossil footprint. These footprints are "motions turned to stone." They show where animals ran or jumped or sat.

Fossil footprints show where a dinosaur walked.

Even the paths to and from their feeding places are evident.

In the American Museum of Natural History in New York, a great dinosaur skeleton is on display. Behind it there is a whole series of dinosaur tracks. The deep impressions of the feet were made in mud that hardened into stone. These fossil footprints were taken up in blocks and laid in the museum as though the reptile had just walked on that path. They give a startling feeling of aliveness to the huge dinosaur skeleton.

Thousands of dinosaur tracks can be seen in the Connecticut River Valley. These are at most two hundred million years old.

But plants and animals are not the only things that have left a fossil record. In one place even the weather was fossilized. That sounds impossible, but it is true. On a certain day, millions of years ago, it rained. Not a long rain, but a short, hard shower. Big drops fell on soft mud and made little holes. The mud baked in the sun. Finally the mud became solid stone which showed the holes made by the driving rain. So the story of a storm was written for those who can read the record of the rocks.

Usually fossilization is a very slow process. Sometimes it takes millions of years. Still, if conditions are just right, it could happen in a few thousand or possibly hundreds of years.

When it comes to hunting fossils, people often ask, "How do you know where to dig?" The answer is, you don't dig—or at least not often. The fossil hunter must first find sedimentary rocks. Then the rocks must be bare. Deserts and dry areas are best because there is little surface grass or vegetation to cover the rock. Also dry country is often cut into ravines and gullies by flash floods or winds and frost and rain. These cuts are helpful because they show a cross section of the earth. When you walk along the sides of a gully or ravine, you may see

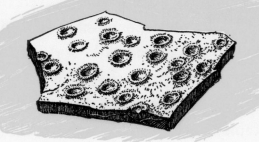

Heavy raindrops made little holes in soft mud which later became solid rock.

23

fossil bones which are partly exposed. These can be carefully uncovered with whisk brooms and small instruments.

The study of fossils has been carried on for only about one hundred and fifty years. At first most fossil bones were found by accident. But about the year 1800, a great French naturalist, Georges Cuvier, became seriously interested in studying fossils. He collected many bones and wrote scientific papers about them. It may be said that he was the founder of the science of paleontology, the study of fossils. Literally paleontology means "the science of ancient living things."

Not until the end of the War Between the States was there a real program of fossil collecting in America. At that time the United States government sent out exploring parties into the West. One thing they were to find out was what minerals existed in this little-known region. Nearly every exploring party contained at least one geologist to study the soil, rocks and minerals. During their work, the geologists discovered many fossil bones.

These were of special interest to two scientists: Professor Cope of Philadelphia and Professor Marsh of Yale University. They were both rich men and friends. Each sent out fossil collectors at his own expense between 1870 and 1895. Each studied and named many new animals. But soon personal rivalry developed. The two brilliant scientists seemed to think there weren't enough fossils for everyone. They became bitter enemies.

Nevertheless, their work greatly helped the study of paleontology all over the world. Scientists realized that fossils existed on every continent. If they found similar fossils in different parts of the world, they would know that plant and animal life had been similar. The record of the fossils would give a record of life in the distant past. So museums began to send out expeditions to collect fossils in almost every part of the earth.

Central Asia was one of the last areas to be explored. No one knew whether it contained fossil bones. But scientists did know that many ancient animals of Europe and North America were closely related. Central Asia lies right between the two continents. Perhaps some of the animals of Europe and North America had originated in Central Asia. From this great middle area they may have spread to the other continents.

Some years ago I made up my mind to explore Central Asia, hunting for fossils and other natural-history specimens. The Gobi Desert was the place to begin work. For two thousand miles it stretches east and west right through the center of Mongolia. It is one of the driest and most fearful deserts of the world.

At that time no one had traveled in the Gobi Desert except by camel. But those creatures travel very slowly, averaging only ten miles a day on a long march. I decided to use automobiles instead. Everyone thought the expedition would be a failure and that none of us would return. But the cars were very successful, and we drove many thousands of miles in the desert. There were forty men, eight motor cars, and 150 camels to carry gasoline and supplies. The expedition was made up of some of the best scientists in the world. We discovered great fields of fossils including bones of many unknown animals. As we expected, some of the animals were closely related to those of either Europe or North America or of both continents.

In the book entitled *All About Dinosaurs,* I have told of the dinosaur bones we discovered. Those great creatures lived in the Age of Reptiles, long before mammals dominated the earth.

Motor cars were used for the first time in exploring the Gobi Desert.

We also discovered the fossil bones of many strange beasts that followed the reptiles. In this book I want to tell of these creatures, for they will help to give a picture of the world in the Age of Mammals that followed the Age of Reptiles.

Modern Mammals

All the creatures on this page are classified as mammals. Unlike reptiles, all true mammals have hair, give birth to their young alive, and have warm blood. It is easy to see that mammals are of many kinds, sizes and shapes.

Whale

Bat

Man

Mouse

Giraffe

African elephant

3.

In the Age of Mammals

The Age of Mammals began about seventy-two million years ago when the dinosaurs disappeared. Those great creatures were reptiles—cold-blooded animals closely related to crocodiles and distantly related to snakes and lizards. As they began to vanish, a new type of animal began to appear. These were little creatures no larger than rats. Unlike dinosaurs they were *covered with hair and had warm blood*. Their blood always remained at the same temperature and did not change with heat or cold. The young were carried in the mother's body and were born alive. Their mothers nursed them with milk. They had much bigger and better brains than the stupid dinosaurs.

These animals are called mammals, from *mamma*, the Latin word meaning "breast." Many mammals look very unlike each other. Even so, a whale and a skunk, a giraffe and a bat, an elephant and a mouse, a man and a bear are all mammals.

There are two great groups of mammals. Those that eat grass, leaves and other vegetation are called *herbivores;* those that live chiefly on meat are called *carnivores.* In between is a group that eat both vegetables and meat. These are called *omnivores.* Man is an omnivore. So is a bear.

The Age of Mammals is divided into seven periods. Of course, the number of years in each period cannot be determined exactly. Also, different estimates are being made by different scientists. The latest, given by Dr. George G. Simpson, is as follows:

Periods in the Age of Mammals

Name of Period	Time When Each Period Began	How Long Each Period Lasted
Paleocene Period	72½ million years ago	17½ million years
Eocene or Dawn Period	55 million years ago	20 million years
Oligocene Period	35 million years ago	10 million years
Miocene or Middle Period	25 million years ago	15 million years
Pliocene Period	10 million years ago	10 million years
Pleistocene Period (Includes the Ice Age)	1 million years ago	1 million years
Recent Period	25 thousand years ago	25 thousand years

A great variety of creatures have lived in the Age of Mammals. Some of them were as strange looking as dinosaurs. One kind grew to enormous size. Its body was as long as a school bus and as big as two buses piled on top of each other. It could eat leaves from the very tops of trees. Another was a huge wolflike animal. No other flesh-eating mammal ever reached such a terrifying size. One fantastic beast had a head like a horse but great claws instead of hoofs. There were lions and tigers and hyenas, and huge bears that lived in caves.

A strange, long-haired kind of elephant, called the mammoth, lived near the edge of the ice. And in the same snowy region lived the woolly rhinoceros.

Some mammals, such as horses and rhinoceroses, are known to have lived fifty or sixty millions of years ago. As climate and food gradually changed, they were able to adapt themselves. As a result, their descendants are still living today. But these descendants are very different from their early ancestors.

Through the years some mammals grew bigger with each generation. The present ones are the biggest of their group. The horse is an example of a mammal which was once very small and is now quite large. Most of the mammals were very small in the beginning. After thousands of years some got so big that they couldn't move about easily or get enough food. So each generation began to get smaller than earlier generations. Finally they reached the proper size at which they could survive.

Many other kinds of mammals lived for a few million years and then died out. Why they died, no one knows. They have no descendants existing today.

During the Age of Reptiles the climate and the surface of the earth were much the same everywhere. There were few high mountains. Great shallow inland seas existed where there is now dry land. The dinosaurs didn't have to worry about cold weather which no reptiles like, for the land was mostly low, hot and humid all year.

But by the beginning of the Age of Mammals, everything was different. The whole world began to change. Of course, the changes took place very, very, very slowly. But every year things were a little different from what they had been the year before.

The climate was no longer the same all over the earth. Some places were temperate like northern California today; others were really cold. But in the south it was still warm and hot.

Instead of all lowlands, there were hills and high meadows. Hardwood forests grew where there had been jungles of palm and fig trees. The great inland seas dried up. So did many of the rivers and marshes.

During the Eocene and Oligocene periods, the first part of the Age of Mammals, the surface of the land did not change very greatly. But in the middle or Miocene period about twenty million years ago, there were many changes. Great mountain systems began to rise in some places. In what is now Tibet, the Himalaya Mountains pushed up, cutting off the rains and moist winds. Beyond the mountains, forests disappeared and streams and grass dried up. Central Asia became a desert. It was no longer a land of plenty and easy travel for animals. As a result many mammals died. They simply could not adjust themselves to the changed conditions.

All through the Age of Mammals, the geography of the world has changed continually. At certain times some of the continents were separated. At other times they were connected. In certain periods a land bridge joined Asia and North America across the Bering Strait. Sometimes the land sank, and the bridge was broken. Then, after a while, the ocean bed rose again, and once more

Elephant   Bison   Sloth

At one time continents were connected by land bridges, shown on this map as shaded areas. Many early mammals could travel by land from one continent to another. Elephants, bison and sloths traveled from Europe and Asia to America. Camels, horses and llamas traveled from America to Asia and Europe.

Llama

Horse

Camel

35

land connected the two continents. Mammals, and probably early men, walked back and forth between Siberia and Alaska.

During the last part of the Age of Reptiles, North and South America were connected as they are today. Then the land bridge that we called the Isthmus of Panama disappeared. For about sixty million years South America remained an island continent. About five or six million years ago the two continents were joined again by Middle, or Central, America. They have remained so ever since.

At one time Asia and Australia were connected by way of Malaya and the East Indies. Africa and Europe were joined broadly at the Mediterranean Sea.

Most scientists agree that various land connections between continents have existed during the past fifty million years. As proof they point to the fossils that have been found on the various continents. Fossil bones show that some of the animals of one continent are closely related to animals of another. That couldn't be unless the animals had been able to travel back and forth between continents. It would have been impossible for many of them to go by sea, so there must have been land bridges

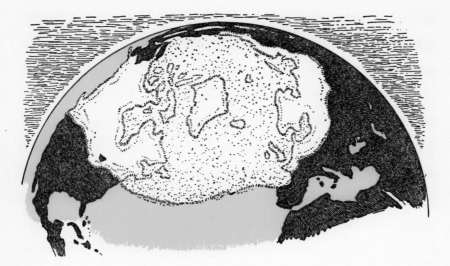

Ice Age glaciers pushed into Europe and North America.

connecting the continents as North and South America are connected now.

During the last million years, in the Pleistocene period, world climate suffered a great change. This was the period of the Ice Age. No one really knows what caused the Ice Age. But we do know that the climate of much of the world became bitterly cold.

In western Europe and parts of America, glaciers pushed down from the north at various times. Then the land was overlaid with ice thousands of feet thick. It was like the icecaps of Greenland and the Antarctic continent today. There were three or four of these cold glacial periods. Each one continued for thousands of years. But in between there were even longer warm stages known as inter-glacial periods. The ice retreated for the last time somewhere between fifteen and twenty-five thousand years ago. Possibly we are in a warm, inter-glacial stage right now. Someday there may be another Ice Age. But no one can predict for sure. Man's life and records are too short for us to know.

It is not difficult to understand how glaciers are made. When snow piles up faster than it melts, the weight of the snow turns it to ice. During the winter there may be heavy snow which piles up in drifts. If the summer is either too cool or too short, the snow will not melt entirely. After a while, the drifts get so deep and the snow becomes so heavy that the weight turns it into solid ice.

Where the ground is level, ice sheets are formed. In the valleys between the mountain slopes, frozen rivers or glaciers appear. As a rule, these glaciers push through the valleys very slowly. But in the polar regions they may move fifty feet a day. Usually the speed is a little greater in summer than in winter. It is faster in the warm day-time than at night. There are many small glaciers in existence today so we can watch them as they change.

As the vast glaciers of the Ice Age pushed forward, such cold-loving animals as the reindeer, the woolly mammoth, and the woolly rhinoceros were pushed far south of their original homes. We know this was the case because we have found their fossil bones. These fossils tell us where certain animals traveled.

The animals that stayed in the cold areas had to grow thick coats of hair to keep themselves warm. Some mammals couldn't adapt themselves to the changed conditions and became extinct.

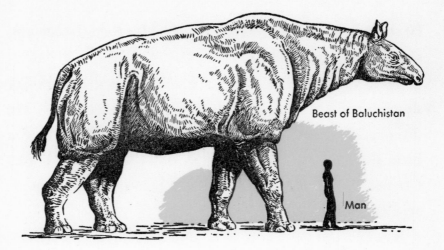

Beast of Baluchistan

Man

4.

The Beast of Baluchistan

One of the strange beasts of the past is known to scientists as the Beast of Baluchistan. It lived about twenty to thirty million years ago. But for thousands of years it had not been seen on the earth.

Then in 1911 the late Sir Clive Forster Cooper went to India to hunt for fossils in a place called Baluchistan. He found three neck bones and part of the leg and foot bones of a gigantic mammal. Never had such huge bones been discovered! There wasn't enough evidence to show what kind of a mammal it was. Cooper guessed it might be some form of rhinoceros and named it *Baluchitherium*, the Beast of Baluchistan.

Four years later, a Russian geologist named Borissiak dug up a fossil mammal of similar astounding size. He discovered its bones in northern Turkestan. He found a little more of his mammal than did Cooper. And, like Cooper, he thought that perhaps it belong to the rhinoceros family.

Since he did not know of Cooper's discovery, Borissiak named his mammal *Indricotherium* for the Indrik beast, a fairy-tale monster described in a Russian legend. According to the old tales, the Indrik beast could walk, run and fly above the clouds. When it walked, the earth was said to tremble under its enormous feet. Evidently Borissiak thought that the fossil mammal he had unearthed must have made the earth shake when it walked.

But even after these discoveries, scientists were puzzled. What kind of beast could have had such huge bones? When did it live and where? We only knew that it must have been a giant, the biggest mammal that ever walked the earth. But the rest was a mystery. I was lucky enough to help solve that mystery on my expedition to the Gobi Desert in 1922.

All About Strange Beasts of the Past

Soon after we arrived in April Dr. Walter Granger, one of our party, discovered two enormous foot bones. He suspected that they belonged to a mammal like the Beast of Baluchistan. But we found nothing more of that sort until August fourth. Then we were camped in the very center of the Gobi Desert.

One of our Chinese chauffeurs, named Wang, was waiting for Dr. Granger out in the desert. He decided to do a little prospecting on his own account. Within ten minutes Wang discovered a huge fossil bone in the bottom of a gully. With great pride he showed Dr. Granger the bone. It proved to be the end of an upper foreleg. Other parts could be seen in the sand. One was the side of a lower jaw with teeth as big as apples. The bones had become fossilized, and Dr. Granger was able to take them out easily. Late in the evening he and Wang reached camp bringing the mysterious fossil bones. We were all very excited. Sitting about the table, we studied the fossils. None of us had seen such enormous mammal bones. Surely they must belong to the Beast of Baluchistan. Still, they did not tell us positively what creature it was, although the teeth resembled those of a rhinoceros.

"If only we could find a skull," said Dr. Granger,

Dr. Granger and Wang carried the great fossil bone to camp.

"we'd know for sure. But the skull must have been broken up. We hunted all around the place. We brought back every scrap of bone that showed."

About midnight we blew out the candles and crawled into our fur sleeping bags. I didn't sleep very well. *Baluchitheriums* were lumbering through my mind all night. I had a vivid dream. In it, I found a complete skull of the Beast in the bottom of the ravine.

Next morning I told Dr. Granger of my dream. I couldn't get it out of my mind. I said I wanted to go back to the place with Wang and have a look myself. Dr. Granger laughed. "I don't think your dream will come true," he said. "But why not go? It might be well to dig where Wang found the bones, even if you don't see any."

So I drove back with Wang and Shackelford, the photographer. Both of them had brought shovels. While they dug in the bottom of the gully, I walked up one side. In about three minutes I reached the top of the ridge and looked down the other side. Instantly, I saw a piece of bone in the bottom of the wash. Its black and white color was unmistakable. With a yell I leaped down the steep slope. Shackelford and Wang came around the corner on the run. I was on my knees scratching like a terrier. Already a huge chunk of bone had been exposed. Other pieces showed in the sand. They were completely fossilized and very hard. There was no danger of breaking them! In our excitement we dug so fast that the sand flew in all directions. We unearthed one chunk of bone after another.

Suddenly my fingers struck a huge block. Shackelford followed it down and found the other end. Soon he located a giant tooth. There was no doubt then. We had discovered a skull of the Beast of Baluchistan!

One end of the block was loose and easily removed. The rest extended far back into the sand. When Shackelford found another tooth, I knew it was time to stop. Dr. Granger was the one to take over the work.

At six o'clock we burst into camp as the men were having tea. Granger could hardly believe it when I told him my dream had come true. We produced the fossils we had been able to bring back. Almost with awe, the scientists studied our find.

All of us had realized that the Beast of Baluchistan was a colossal creature. But the size of the bones left us absolutely astounded. We had brought in only the front of the skull with several teeth. But that was enough for Dr. Granger. "I'm sure," he said, "that the Beast is a giant, *hornless* rhinoceros. It isn't like any other animal known to science."

For three days, four of us worked at "Baluch Ravine," as we named the place. The skeleton had lain near the point where two gullies met. As heavy rains came down and the earth weathered away, the bones fell away from each other. Part of the skeleton had gone down one side of the slope. That was what Wang found the first day. The rest had rolled down the other side where I discovered it.

Dr. Granger worked on the partly buried skull. The rest of us searched the desert at the outlet of the ravine. We shifted every foot of sand in the bottom of the two gullies. Many bits of bone were recovered. Shackelford picked up fragments 'way out on the plain where they had been washed during a flash flood.

After the skull was exposed, Granger soaked strips of burlap in flour paste. He worked the wet cloth into every crevice of the skull. When all of it had been covered, he left it to dry. The burlap became a hard shell and thus protected the bone. Later on the burlap was easily removed with water.

Actually the skull was in 360 fragments. These had to be packed with the greatest care and carried by camel 1,500 miles over the desert. Then they journeyed 8,000 miles across the Pacific Ocean and the continent of North America to the American Museum of Natural History in New York. There the parts had to be fitted together like the pieces of a jigsaw puzzle and missing pieces had to be built up in plaster. It took four months to restore the skull and jaws of the Beast of Baluchistan.

After unearthing that first skull, we made a second extraordinary discovery of the *Baluchitherium*. The credit belongs to another Chinese, Liu Hsi-kou. His sharp eyes caught the glint of white bone in the yellow sand of a steep hillside. He dug a little and then reported to Dr. Granger who dug some more. To his amazement, he found the foot and lower leg of a "Baluch." *It was standing upright* just as if the Beast had carelessly left it behind when he took another step. Fossils are seldom found in this position. There was only one explanation for this —quicksand!

It was the right hind leg that Liu had found. Granger estimated that the right foreleg would be about twelve feet down the slope. He measured the distance and began to dig. Sure enough there it was. A huge bone like the trunk of a fossil tree standing erect. After that it was easy to find the two legs on the left side.

All four legs were soon exposed, each one in its separate pit. It was an amazing sight. I sat down on a hilltop looking at them. My imagination drifted back thirty million years to the day when the tragedy must have happened. It was plainly told by the great stumps. Probably

All four legs of a "Baluch" were soon exposed, each in its own pit.

the Beast had come to drink in a stream. Suddenly its forefeet had sunk in quicksand just as the saber-toothed tiger sank in the soft tar. Bellowing in terror, it must have settled back a little on its haunches. With desperate struggles it tried to free its feet from the gripping sands. It sank rapidly, fighting to the end. Only when the golden sands filled its throat and nose did it die. If it had been only partly buried, it would have died of starvation and the body would have fallen on its side. How wonderful it would have been if we could have found the whole fossil skeleton standing upright! That would have been something for the world to wonder at.

Evidently we had missed getting a complete skeleton by just about twenty thousand years. The enclosing rock had been slowly cut away by the knives of wind, frost and rain. Bit by bit the bones went with it. They lay scattered in hundreds of pieces on the valley floor.

Twenty or thirty million years ago, many of the Beasts must have lived in this region. They had no enemies to kill them and the food conditions must have been excellent. Otherwise, the Beasts couldn't have grown so large. We found a dozen places where the great bones had crumbled as the rocks wore away.

In 1928, on a later expedition, Shackelford discovered part of another skeleton. One day he walked into camp for luncheon, looking like the cat that had swallowed the canary. He remarked casually that he had found a bone. It sounded too casual, I thought. I was sure half the story had not been told.

"Come on, Shack," I said, "tell us all."

"Oh, you wouldn't be interested. It's just a bone."

"Is it a big bone?"

"Well, yes. I'd say it was big."

"How big?"

"About the size of my body."

A shout went up from the table at that, for Shack's body is far from thin. A bone as big as his body would be *some* bone.

"If you don't believe me," he said, "I'll show you."

And show us he did. The place was two miles from camp. It proved to be a gray slope that dropped sharply into a deep ravine. Ten feet down the side lay a great white ball. I could hardly believe my eyes. It actually *was* as big as Shack's body! A little brushing off of yellow sand showed it to be the head of the humerus, or upper foreleg bone. More brushing exposed its entire length. Also another massive shaft lay beside it.

All of us stared in amazement. It was not easy to surprise Walter Granger when it came to fossils. He had seen too many of them. But this really gave him a jolt. As for me, I was speechless.

The upper foreleg bone which Shack had found was four feet long. A man's arm bone would look like a sliver beside it. The second shaft proved to be the radius, or lower foreleg bone. It was five feet long and so heavy that two men could hardly lift it. Truly, this was the leg of a giant! To get it out we would have to dig away part of the hillside. A whole skeleton might be there!

Beast of
Baluchistan

When the Beast of Baluchistan stretched out its nose, it must
have been 25 feet above the ground.

The Beast of Baluchistan

We found that this Beast had died in the bed of a very swift stream. The flesh decayed, and the skeleton fell apart. Some of the smaller bones had been washed away, but the massive leg bones were too heavy for the torrent to move them.

In addition to the leg bones we found several great ribs and part of a jaw. It was disappointing not to find the skull. But two other Baluch skulls were discovered later near this same place.

Although the bones we found belonged to different beasts, we could use them to build up a complete skeleton. We made this skeleton the basis for modeling the flesh in clay. From the first, the Beast of Baluchistan seemed unbelievably large. It was hard to realize that such a huge creature ever did live. From nose to tail it measured 34 feet. That is longer than a school bus. At the shoulder it was 17 feet 9 inches high—higher than two school buses piled one on top of the other. When the neck stretched out, its nose would have been 25 feet above the ground. That is about nine feet higher than the tallest giraffe. A six-foot man, standing under the Beast, could hardly touch its stomach. Even the great dinosaur, *Brontosaurus*, the Thunder Lizard of the Age of Reptiles, was no larger in body, although it had a much longer neck and tail.

As Dr. Granger suspected, the Beast of Baluchistan proved to be a giant hornless rhinoceros. Today all rhinoceroses have horns on their noses. They use them for fighting and protection. But the Beast of Baluchistan was so big that no other animal could harm it. Moreover, at the very front of its upper jaw it had two thick teeth that projected downward.

Some scientists think that the Beast ate leaves, twigs and buds from the treetops like a giraffe. With such high shoulders and such a long neck, it could have reached the highest branches. And its two great teeth would have been useful in hooking down branches or in fighting with others of his kind.

The Beast of Baluchistan lived in the Oligocene and Miocene periods, twenty to thirty million years ago. Possibly even earlier than that, his ancestors branched off from the main stem of the rhinoceros family. They formed a new branch of their own. Instead of horns for protection, they developed great size.

Many millions of years ago, the climate was warm on the central Asian plateau. At that time this part of the world was not very high. The country was open and had streams, rivers and lush grass. While it was not heavily forested, it did have a number of trees.

When the Himalaya Mountains rose, they acted like a wall and cut off the warm winds carrying moisture. The land in Central Asia dried up and the trees disappeared. Everything changed. The Beast of Baluchistan had to change, too, if he was to survive. He had to accommodate himself to the new conditions. Of course, he could have left the country if he had not been too big to travel. He needed so much food for his great body that he couldn't survive and couldn't change. So eventually he and all his close relatives died out. They never got out of Asia. He was what scientists call too highly specialized—too completely adapted for a special kind of life.

Woolly
rhinoceros

5.

The Wandering Rhinoceros

About fifty million years ago, in the Eocene or Dawn period, rhinoceroses roamed the western plains of North America in countless thousands. Strangely enough our modern rhinos are descended from the same primitive group of animals that also gave rise to the horse and the tapir. Probably that remote ancestor was a timid little five-toed creature, but its bones have never been found.

The first rhinos were little fellows, too small to fight their enemies. They simply ran away when danger threatened. Some of them stayed in water a good deal of the time. The streams were reasonably safe, and the plants and leaves of near-by trees were very tasty.

This group of water-loving rhinos, called *amynodonts*, started in what we now call Wyoming. But they seemed to want to try new ponds and streams in far-off places. So they began to wander. In the next twenty million years they splashed their way from Wyoming up to Alaska. Then they went across the land bridge which, at that time, connected North America and Asia.

Until 1922 no one knew how far into Asia the Wyoming rhino had gone. But that year we found fossil bones of the rhinoceros in the Gobi Desert. It was a great discovery, but it came quite by chance. Because it shows how scientists work when hunting fossils, I will quote what I wrote in my field journal on that expedition.

"*September 7, 1922*. Two days after leaving the Well of the Sweet Waters, we crossed a long stretch of gravel desert. It was almost without life. No plants, no animals. Only a few spotted lizards. That was all.

"Finally we came into a great basin. It was more than a hundred miles wide. In the distance, the blue line of an enormous bluff showed against the sky. It looked like fossil ground. I pulled up to the base and signaled the others to stop.

"The Mongols made camp while we scattered over the sides of the bluff. Almost at once we found pieces of bones. An hour later I walked around a big rock. Shackelford, our photographer, was on his knees near the top of the bluff. He was scratching at the earth with his little pickaxe. He had discovered some big bones. Dr. Granger, our paleontologist, recognized them as bones of the water-loving rhinoceros. It was a very important find.

"Soon Dr. Berkey, the geologist, came up. He had been studying the side of the bluff for some time. He said he had traced the bed of an ancient stream. Thirty or forty million years ago, it had run on the surface of the ground.

"It was easy to follow the course that ancient stream had taken. We were looking at a cross section of it. At the bottom were heavy rocks, then coarse gravel. Above that, small pebbles, sand and fine silt. All were in layers and showed perfectly.

"Near the bones Shackelford had found, there was a sharp drop in the course of the stream bed. At the foot of the drop was a mass of pebbles and large stones. Millions of years ago there must have been a pool at the bottom of a waterfall tumbling over a small ledge. An animal that had died in the upper part of the stream would have been carried into the pool. There it would have settled down and would have been covered with sand. Dr. Berkey said we ought to dig there. Almost certainly we'd find bones.

"I scooped away the sand with a small spade. In five minutes I had located a jawbone. Directly below it was a skull. Shackelford found a fine, unbroken jaw two feet away.

"For three days we remained to dig at the foot of this great bluff. Every time Dr. Granger started to remove a skull, he found another near it. The ancient site of the pool was full of fossil bones. Almost all of them were of the water-loving rhinoceros. This type was new to science. The stream must have been alive with turtles also, for we discovered dozens of fossilized turtle shells, large and small.

"We had to hurry because it was getting late in the season. Any day we might be trapped by one of the terrible Mongolian blizzards. Dr. Granger spent almost every daylight hour in 'The Hole', as we named the fossil pool. At first he welcomed human vistors. But sooner or later everyone did something wrong, and we were told

Into every crevice of the bone, Granger worked the burlap
that had been soaked in flour paste.

not to bother him again. Finally, only our dog Mushka
and our two pet crows remained to keep him company.
On the second day, Mushka tipped over a tray of bones,
and Granger sent him away.

"The two crows behaved fairly well. They were most
amusing, for they liked to eat the flour paste Dr. Granger
was using to cover the bones. They would get their glossy

black feathers so completely stuck up that they could hardly fly.

"But at last one of them committed an unpardonable sin. Granger had taken out a beautiful rhino skull. It was absolutely perfect except for a tiny piece of bone from one side. After an hour's sifting of sand, he found it and carefully pasted it in position. The moment his back was turned, one of the crows hopped on the skull, picked off the piece of bone and swallowed it. Dr. Granger never forgave the bird. When we got back to Peking, he was still grumbling about it as he packed the skull for shipment to New York."

The water-loving rhinoceroses lived for approximately twenty million years. Then they all disappeared in both North America and Asia.

For millions of years the main stem of the rhinoceros family remained in North America. Their fossil bones have been found in Maryland, the Carolinas and Florida as well as in the West. Apparently these rhinos were able to adapt themselves to changes in climate and the coming and going of forests and even mountains. Their bodies changed too, getting bigger and bigger.

We think that branches of this main stem migrated to Asia, Europe and Africa. But apparently they never got to South America even though skeletons have been found in Nicaragua. Neither did they reach the island continent of Australia.

At some time, possibly five or ten million years ago, one branch of the rhinoceros tribe wandered north. Up there it was getting colder every year, so these rhinoceroses began to grow a thick coat of hair to keep themselves warm. This didn't happen quickly because the Ice Age was very slow in coming. But eventually the woolly rhinoceros was clothed much like the woolly mammoth. Both animals lived at the same time and in many of the same places.

We know a good deal about the woolly rhinoceros. The Polish Academy of Science has several specimens that may be ten to twenty-five thousand years old. They are as carefully preserved as if they had been embalmed by an undertaker. Apparently these creatures had been drowned in a swift stream during the third Ice Age. Their carcasses were washed ashore near what is now Starunia, Poland. Gradually they were covered by sand and clay. But crude oil and salt were mixed with the clay.

This preserved the bodies so perfectly that we can almost imagine they are alive.

In addition to these well-preserved specimens, we also have magnificent drawings made by men who lived fifteen to twenty thousand years ago. These are the drawings of Cro-Magnon man on the cave walls in France and Spain. They show us just how the woolly rhinoceros looked in real life.

From the cave paintings we know that the woolly rhino was covered with thick under wool and long brown outer hair. Its square upper lip would permit it to graze on herbs and grass that lived under the snow. Its long narrow head had an enormous front horn and a shorter rear horn.

The painting of a woolly rhinoceros on the wall of a cave.

The mammoth must have fallen into a crack in the glacier.

6.

A Cold-Storage Mammoth

The mammoth is one of the most interesting prehistoric animals we know anything about. It was a kind of elephant that sometimes grew to be twelve feet tall. On each side of its great trunk were long, curved tusks.

The word *mammoth* is derived from the Tartar word *mamma* meaning "the earth." That seemed a good name, I suppose, because natives of Siberia found mammoth bones buried in the earth. From this some mistakenly came to believe that the great beast had always lived underground, burrowing like a big mole. And they were sure it died when it came to the surface and breathed fresh air!

There have been no living mammoths for thousands of years. But scientists have learned a great deal about them. Much of this information was gathered from fossil remains. Probably the most important find was the discovery of a completely frozen mammoth which is known as the Berezovka mammoth. It had lain frozen in Siberia for many thousands of years. When it was found in 1901, its hair and flesh, even its clotted blood and the food in its stomach were perfectly preserved. The frozen ground in which it had been buried had kept it in as good condition as would any deep freeze today.

Years later I saw the mounted skin of the Berezovka mammoth in Russia at the Leningrad Museum of Natural History. And its story was told to me by one of the men who helped bring the great prehistoric monster out of Siberia.

"Without doubt," he said, "the beast had fallen into a crevasse, or crack, in a glacier. Some such cracks are hundreds of feet deep. Perhaps the mammoth was crossing a snow bridge that broke under its weight. Anyway, it must have had quite a long fall, for the hip, or pelvis, and the right foreleg were broken.

"As it struggled in the crevasse, tons of snow and ice were probably brought down upon its body. Actually it put itself in cold storage. It remained frozen for I don't know how many centuries.

"Finally the icecap over the land melted. Still the mammoth lay buried in frozen earth. After a while some of the ground about its body weathered away. The head and foreleg were exposed. As the sun warmed the flesh, it began to decay. It gave out a horrible odor. This attracted dogs. Through them, natives discovered the mammoth. This was in 1901.

"The Museum at St. Petersburg, now Leningrad, was notified; I was working there in the Department of Preparation. Dr. Otto Hertz told me about it. The Czar was much interested and ordered an expedition to be organized to collect the mammoth. Dr. Hertz was in charge, and he asked me to go.

"We had a long sledge journey, but at last we got to the village of Berezovka near which the mammoth had been discovered. We had heard that the smell was awful. It was! When we began work the first day, none of us thought we could stand it. But the Czar had ordered that the mammoth be prepared for the Museum. We had to go ahead whether we wanted to or not. We didn't dare go back to the Czar and tell him we couldn't get his mammoth because it smelled too bad. I don't know what would have happened to us if we had. The natives didn't have any choice, either. They had to help us or be imprisoned.

"After we got the soft, stinking flesh cut away, the rest wasn't so bad. We took out the whole carcass piece by piece. Some of the meat looked just like good fresh beef. It was dark red and marbled with fat. We could hardly believe it was thousands of years old. The dogs ate the meat and enjoyed it.

"The layer of fat beneath the skin was white, without odor and four inches thick. That mammoth had eaten well. The frozen blood looked like solid bits of potassium permanganate. When melted they turned into dark red spots.

"The stomach contained twenty-seven pounds of undigested food: fir cones, bits of larch and pine trees, sedge, wild thyme, several flowers and two kinds of moss. So now there is no guesswork about what food the mammoths ate.

"Unlike any living elephant, the body was covered with soft, woolly, yellowish fur. This was under a thick outer bristle-like coat. These long hairs protected the mammoth from rain and snow. The woolly underfur kept it warm even in bitter cold. Some of the outer hairs were fourteen inches long and dark rust-brown. Thick, stiff hairs formed massive patches on the flanks, belly, shoulders, cheeks and chin.

"We skinned the mammoth, then packed the skin, the skeleton and parts of the inside anatomy on twenty dog sledges. The dogs pulled it nearly two thousand miles to the town of Irkutsk on the Trans-Siberian Railway.

"As we followed along on our sledges, I thought of the time when the great mammoth had roamed over this very same country. That was in the gloomy days of the Ice Age. There would have been more snow and ice than now, but we know that mammoths liked cold. Now, after all these centuries, we were taking its skin and bones to a railroad. Certainly no train ever carried more unusual freight!

"In the Museum, I helped mount the skin. We posed it in a half sitting position just as the mammoth was found."

Since the discovery of the Berezovka mammoth, others have been found in Siberia and Alaska. But none was so perfectly preserved as that first specimen. Occasionally parts of frozen mammoths are uncovered in mining operations today. Some people eat the meat just to say they have done it. At a dinner of the Explorers' Club in New York, some years ago, chunks of mammoth meat were flown down from Alaska. They were served as hors d'oeuvres.

Largely because of these frozen specimens we know exactly what the woolly mammoth looked like. Its body shape was very different from the living African and Indian elephants. The head was crowned with a mass of long hair. A deep hollow marked the neck. A great hump on its back was composed entirely of fat. The animal could live on this fat by absorbing it when there was no food. A camel's hump serves the same purpose. The hindquarters of the mammoth sloped rapidly downward to a short tail.

The ancient mammoth had much larger tusks than any living elephant. The tusks are the animal's upper front teeth which have grown to great size and are used for fighting and digging up roots to eat. Those of the woolly mammoth were from eight to ten feet in length. But one tusk found in Alaska measured almost thirteen feet. The tusks were strongly curved inward. Sometimes, in old age, these tusks completely crossed each other. Then they were of no use for fighting or getting food.

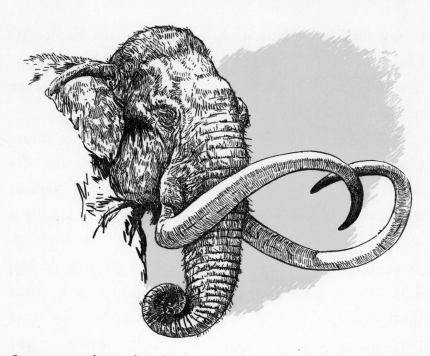

Sometimes the tusks of an old mammoth crossed each other.

For thousands of years, natives of Siberia and Alaska have been finding bones of the woolly mammoth. Even today they gather the tusks and sell them as ivory. As far back as 250 B.C. mammoth ivory was being sold to the Chinese by Siberian natives. Records show that about 50,000 of these tusks have been sold in China during the last 250 years. We can only guess how many tusks have been dug up in Siberia alone. Certainly it would be in the hundreds of thousands.

The woolly mammoth was by no means the largest of the mammoth tribe. The one that reached the greatest size was the imperial mammoth. The bones of his ancestor have been discovered in Africa, in rocks that are about four million years old. At that time the animal was only four feet eight inches tall.

A million years later that same type had spread to India. Fossils there show that these early creatures had become bigger—about six feet seven inches tall. The ancestors of the imperial mammoth kept growing larger and larger. They continued to travel to other parts of the world.

In the early days of the Ice Age, about 800,000 years ago, they reached France and North America. By that time they were often as tall as twelve feet three inches. But the biggest of all were the ones that lived in what we now call Nebraska, Kansas, Iowa, Texas, California and Mexico at the end of the Ice Age. They reached a height of thirteen to fourteen feet at the shoulder. That is taller than any living elephant.

This imperial mammoth was probably hairless. His teeth, which were adapted to crushing leaves and twigs, show that he must have lived in the forest. As the western forests began to disappear, the imperial mammoth disappeared, too.

Another type of mammoth is referred to as the Columbian mammoth. During the Ice Age it roamed the meadows and forests of western Europe. Then it went on to North America, moving overland by the land bridge from Asia. In America this species is called the Jeffersonian mammoth in honor of President Thomas Jefferson, one of the first Americans to realize the importance of collecting fossils. The Jeffersonian mammoth flourished in the temperate regions of this continent, and its fossil remains are very numerous.

It was not until fifteen or twenty thousand years ago that man crossed the land bridge from Asia to North America. There he found three kinds of mammoths roaming the plains and forests. In the far north was the woolly mammoth. In the temperate parts was the Jeffersonian mammoth. And in the warm southern areas was the great imperial mammoth.

But thousands of years before there were human beings in America, men were well acquainted with mammoths in the Old World. How well they knew them was shown by a remarkable discovery near the town of Predmost in what is now Czechoslavakia.

In 1924 a whole village was unearthed. It had been occupied by mammoth hunters who lived 25,000 years

Frequently, cave men would kill a trapped rhino by dropping stones on its head and body.

ago. In the wintertime these people lived in caves in the hillsides. But in the spring they came to camp on the floors of the valleys. That was because great herds of animals moved through the river valleys in warm weather. They were migrating to the flat plains of Silesia and Poland. So thousands of primitive families gathered for the hunt. Century after century they lived there and hunted. Why they left, no one knows.

But as years went by, a thick blanket of fine, wind-blown dust sifted over their deserted camping grounds. This dust, called "loess," cuts like brown cheese. It buried the mammoth hunters' camp site as completely as the ashes of Mount Vesuvius covered the Italian city of Pompeii. In some places the loess at Predmost reached a depth of sixty-five feet.

The prehistoric village extended over a thousand acres. Not all of it has been uncovered even yet. But it has already given a wonderful picture of the life of our ancestors in the Ice Age.

It was a very orderly village. Certain areas were living quarters. In front of shelters, pitched side by side, were fireplaces. Not far away were the refuse dumps. These contained the fossil bones of mammoths, rhinoceroses, lions, horses, reindeer and arctic foxes. All of the fossil bones were placed in a neat arrangement.

Behind the shelters, three piles of mammoth tusks had been stacked like cord wood. They were separated by a narrow path. At one side was a great field of pelvic bones. Another had only lower jaws.

At first, scientists were puzzled by a half circle of mammoth leg bones. Finally they decided these had been used as fire logs. As the bones heated, the fat oozed out. This kept the fire alight for the primitive hunters.

Of the mammoth skulls which were found, only a few were whole. Evidently hunters had smashed most of them to get at the brains. We know that people of early times loved to eat animal brains—the bigger, the better!

The Predmost men were mighty hunters. But a mammoth or a woolly rhinoceros could not be killed with spears alone. So the men had to find a different method. Across the floor of the valley they dug deep pits and roofed them over with sticks and earth. They looked just like the rest of the ground. But when a mammoth stepped on the roof of a pit, it broke through. The great creature dropped into the hole and was helpless.

Doubtless the hunters were watching. They dragged

up a huge, pear-shaped stone, weighing more than one hundred and twenty pounds. This was tied about with leather thongs. Half a dozen men lifted it and dropped it on the head of the mammoth in the pit. Thus, by his intelligence man conquered the greatest beasts of his age.

During the Ice Age mammoths must have been abundant in all northern continents. We have found enough mammoth bones and frozen mammoths to be sure that great herds existed in Europe and Asia as well as in North America. In caves of France and Spain we have found carvings of the mammoth, too, in ivory and bone. And on these cave walls are pictures of the mammoth drawn by prehistoric men.

Toward the end of the Ice Age, the climate was becoming warmer. The icecap was melting. And as the great ice fields disappeared, the mammoth disappeared, too. Since then he has never been seen alive.

Woolly mammoth

Mastodon

7.

The Fate of the Shovel-Jawed Mastodon

When you look at the picture of a mammoth, you will probably say, "It's some kind of elephant. It has an elephant's trunk." Scientists would agree with you. Except they would probably use the scientific term *proboscis* instead of *trunk*.

Now if you look at the picture of certain kinds of mastodon, you will see that this creature, too, has a trunk or proboscis. At first glance, you may think it is another

Indian elephant

African elephant

Modern elephants are distantly related to mastodons and mammoths.

kind of elephant. Actually the mastodon is only very distantly related to the mammoth and the modern elephant. All three are said to belong to the same family of mammals—the *proboscidea* or "trunk bearers."

In some ways the mastodon was very much like the mammoth. But there are many differences between the two, particularly in the teeth.

Mastodons were of many different kinds. One of the strangest was known as the long-jawed mastodon. It's hard to imagine a creature whose lower jaw was almost as long as the animal was tall. Yet such a beast did exist. One mastodon stood eight feet high at the shoulders. And its lower jaw measured six feet seven inches in length. With such a lower jaw, the trunk could not swing down in true elephant fashion. Instead, the proboscis of the long-jawed mastodon was shorter and was used chiefly to reach upward.

Like the other proboscideans, mastodons were wanderers. They traveled to every continent of the world except Australia. Some forty million years ago they started in North Africa. Gradually they spread to Arabia, all over Europe, Mongolia, Siberia, across the land bridge to North America, and through Central America to South America. Their travels lasted millions of years. We have been able to trace the route by the fossil bones that have been unearthed along the way.

On my Central Asiatic Expedition of 1928, we had an interesting experience trying to identify some of these bones. The region was completely unexplored. We had been driving over a hard gravel plain and stopped on the brink of a great depression. Suddenly a big gray wolf dashed over the edge and across the plain. I grabbed my rifle and rolled him over in full run. There we pitched our tents and set up camp. Below us spread a weird view of red and gray ravines and hills. Far across the basin, sheer cliffs showed like a wall of purple and gold. The plain stretching behind our camp was almost terrifying in its vastness. We named the place Wolf Camp.

All around us there were plenty of fossil bones as well as wolves. Also we found quantities of fossil clam shells —layer upon layer of them. Evidently we were on the edge of what had been a big fresh-water lake. The old shoreline could be seen easily. Probably there had been bogs and quicksand along the water's edge. These would have trapped animals four or five million years ago just as the La Brea tar pits have done more recently. We followed the clam shell layer which marked the shoreline.

One day I was with Dr. Granger, our chief paleontologist. Suddenly a bit of white bone caught my eye. Brushing away the sand, I exposed a great molar tooth. This was mastodon without a doubt! A few moments later Granger turned over a flat stone block. It was like lifting a trap door. Under it lay another tooth firmly set in bone. Using a whisk broom, Dr. Granger followed it down and exposed a skull. The skulls of most proboscideans are very short and wide. This one had a long narrow front. On either side it carried a slender round tusk. Except for the teeth and tusks, we would never have guessed this was the skull of an ancient mastodon.

One day Captain Hill brought in two flat plates that looked like ivory. They were eight inches wide and half an inch thick. Dr. Granger was puzzled.

"They're teeth, all right, but what kind of an animal wore teeth like those? I can't guess. Some strange beast lived here four or five million years ago. I'd certainly like to know what it looked like."

For a week more plates kept turning up. We had a dozen of them. But no one found them attached to any bone. They were always by themselves.

"Someday we'll find out," Granger said, "and I think we'll have a big surprise. We can't leave here till we know what this beast was."

We did not solve the mystery for two weeks. Then it was by pure chance. Dr. Granger was walking back to camp in the late afternoon. He climbed the steep face of the bluff to the plain on which the tents were pitched. Two feet below the edge he stepped on one of the flat plates. It was firmly fastened in a large bone. After a little work, he realized he had the answer to our puzzle. He came back to get me. All the men in camp, including the Chinese and Mongols, went with us. With a small spade, Granger worked away the soft sediment and followed the bone. It was a jaw. We stood by, breathless with excitement. Two of the flat plates lay side by side fastened together. They were a foot and a half across. Behind them, the jaw widened like a shovel. Then it narrowed and divided into two branches. These held molar teeth.

When Dr. Granger saw them, he said: "The beast is a mastodon. Can't be anything else with those teeth. But what a mastodon! I never dreamed there could be such an animal!"

The jaw was more than five feet long. It was shaped exactly like a two-handed scoop shovel. That is the way the beast must have used it. The fact that we found the mastodon on the shore of the ancient lake gave a clue. Quite probably much vegetation had grown there. Our mastodon must have fed on water plants which he scooped up with his enormous shovel jaw. This jaw was sent back to the American Museum of Natural History in New York where it became one of the Museum's prize exhibits.

Two years later we went back to Wolf Camp. We

wanted to find out more about the great shovel-jawed mastodons. Again our tents were pitched right on the edge of the old lake basin. The next day one of our scientists found a deposit of bones six miles away. There was every indication that it had been a death trap.

We began digging with great interest. At first, we did not know that we had discovered one of the world's most remarkable fossil deposits. I wish you could have been there with us. It was thrilling to open that ancient grave! Out there in the desert, in the year 1930, we worked in brilliant sunshine. But millions of years ago, a tragedy had taken place on that very spot. We could understand just what happened. It was like words cut in a book of stone and left for us to read. Every hour at first, then every day, we turned a new page. This is the story we read:

A quiet little bay ran inland from the main lake. Lush vegetation covered the shores. Floating plants sent their roots down into the soft sticky mud. It was thirty feet wide by fifty feet long and perhaps forty feet deep. It was a great hole in the bottom of the bay.

A mastodon worked his way along the shore. He was a

A shovel-jawed mastodon was trapped and sinking in the mud.

grotesque creature. He had an elephant's body. But a short, heavy upper lip overhung a huge shovel-like jaw. Two short, round tusks projected downward on either side. No other beast in all the world looked like him. The mastodon was hungry. He scooped up great quantities of plants in his shovel-shaped lower jaw. He might get a bushel or more at one time. Some he didn't like. Those his big tongue pushed out of the shovel. But the juicy tubers were tucked back into his mouth. The massive molar teeth ground them up into a soft mass.

But the best tubers grew in a thick bed a little distance from shore. That was all right. He could wade to them easily enough. The water only reached his belly when he got to the floating tubers. He settled back on his haunches, and for half an hour stood in one place feeding greedily.

At last his stomach was full, and he wanted to go back to shore. It would be nice to stand in the shade of a tree and drowse for a while. But, strangely enough, he couldn't lift his legs. All four of them were held in clinging mud. At first he was only surprised. Nothing before had ever challenged his strength. He'd give a heave and get out. He gave a heave, but he didn't get out. Instead, his legs sank deeper and deeper into the mud. Sheer terror possessed his brain. Frantically he struggled. The more he fought, the deeper he was engulfed in the mire of death. Frenzied trumpetings echoed from the high shores.

At last they ended in exhausted gurgles as the great beast sank beneath the surface of the water.

Another mastodon came, and still another. Each one died as this one had died. Twenty, we know, were trapped—probably more than that. Down in the green mud, tons of flesh decayed. It fell away from the skeletons leaving the bones to separate, one by one. Some bones were crushed and broken when other victims piled upon them. Some remained as perfect as when they bore the living flesh.

Perhaps at last the death trap was full to overflowing. Perhaps the water, fouled by decaying flesh, sickened the vegetable life. Then the trap would lie unbaited. Perhaps the little bay itself just dried up from lack of rain. Whatever the cause, we know that the lake disappeared. Centuries passed into thousands of centuries. The wind blew continually in gales. Countless tons of dust and sand were heaped on the dry lake floor. The shovel-jawed mastodon's grave was buried deeply, hopelessly lost.

Then came a change of climate. Gradually the dry, bitterly cold winds of the Ice Age cut away the sediment in the old lake bed. Bit by bit the soil was swept high in the air. Most of it dropped upon the plains of China, three hundred miles away. That went on for a million years and continues today. The desert is still giving up its surface, being worn down by the unceasing winds of the Gobi Desert. The mastodon's grave had been uncovered at least a century before we found it. Already the upper part of the deposit had disappeared in dust. The exposed bones were destroyed with the sediments.

Still, much remained. A mass of bones lay buried in hard green clay. This was the mud that once filled the pit. The fossils lay like a huge pile of jackstraws. Great scoop jaws were heaped, one upon another, in every possible position. Some stood on end; others were at oblique angles; still others lay almost horizontal. Some of the jaws were perfect and nearly six feet long. The one we had found some two years before was considered to be one of the world's most extraordinary fossils. But now, we had a dozen better jaws right in front of us. Mixed with them were many other bones. Enormous flat shoulder blades, legs, pelvic bones and dozens of ribs lay in a seemingly hopeless jumble.

It was difficult to take out any one bone, for usually part of it ran under some other. Only by finding the topmost ones could we begin work. The bones were badly

Fossilized bones of the shovel-jawed mastodon lay like a huge pile of jackstraws.

preserved. They were filled with only a little mineral matter and were as soft as chalk.

As soon as part of a bone was exposed, it had to be soaked with shellac. This hardened it. Then more of it could be dug out. Next, it was covered with Japanese rice paper and gum arabic, a kind of glue. The paper and gum held loose bits in place. Then the whole surface must be bandaged with strips of burlap soaked in flour paste. In a few hours the paste dried and the bone was enclosed in a hard shell. *For six weeks, ten men worked at the job!*

In another deposit just below camp, one of our men found the back part of a female mastodon. She had died lying on her side. Within the pelvis were the skull and jaws of an unborn baby. The jaw of the baby was about twelve inches long.

Such specimens of any fossil animal are extremely rare and very interesting. They are particularly so in the *proboscideans* because they show the tooth growth. It is unlike that of other mammals. The huge molar teeth grow up and forward. They push out the first teeth so that only two are in use on either side of each jaw at any one time.

In this second deposit the mother mastodon was the only large animal. Most of the others were small. There were foxes, deer and baby mastodons. Apparently this bog was not very deep. The big mammals could get out, but the babies could not. One of the deer had remarkable antlers. They resemble a woman's hand and are just about that size. The antler tines are like small, spread fingers.

When our work at the pits was finished, we gazed with satisfaction at the pile of specimens. There was very little they had not told us about the skeleton of the shovel-jawed mastodon.

The mastodon that is best known to people is the American mastodon. Its fossil bones have been found over much of the United States and in northern and western Canada. Thousands of teeth and jaws and parts of skeletons tell us a great deal about this strange beast.

Sometimes the American mastodon had two little tusks in the lower jaw as well as the two big ones in the upper jaw. The big tusks curved upward and inward. Usually these big tusks were seven or eight feet long, but one specimen had tusks nine feet long.

A huge deposit of mastodon bones was found near St. Louis, Missouri, where several hundred animals had died in or near the river. Evidently their bodies had been swept downstream in a flood. They landed in a backwater or eddy. The bones were piled up in a great mass and partly fossilized. Some of the bones kept much of their animal matter.

New York State has given us some of the best-preserved mastodons. Probably this is due to the series of meadows, bogs and pools just west of the Catskills. These mark the positions of ancient swamps. They formed after the melting of the ice sheet that once covered eastern North America. Evidently mastodons were trapped in these swamps and sank in the mud. It was just what had happened to the shovel-jawed mastodon in Mongolia. Even today, New York farmers occasionally dig up mastodon bones as they plow. Parts of more than a hundred skeletons have been discovered in New York State alone. One of them is among the most interesting, most traveled, and most important of all fossils. Its story is a real believe-it-or-not tale.

You wouldn't think that the mounted skeleton of an animal as big as an elephant could disappear without a trace. Or that it would be discovered after a hundred years on the other side of the Atlantic Ocean. Nor would you expect that the people who have it never knew that it had been lost and mourned by paleontologists! Well, all of that happened to what is known as Peale's mastodon.

This was the first nearly complete mastodon skeleton ever found in America. Also, it was the first to be mounted here. The bones were discovered in 1799 on John Martin's farm near Newburgh, Orange County,

The Fate of the Shovel-Jawed Mastodon

New York. A well-known painter, Charles Willson Peale, heard about the mastodon bones and became very much interested. He bought them and dug for more in the same place. Eventually he found enough so that his son, Rembrandt Peale, could mount the skeleton for exhibit in Peale's Museum in Philadelphia. Rembrandt Peale was also an artist. While the digging was going on, he made a painting of the scene. It is now in the Boston Museum of Fine Arts.

The painting shows twenty-one men and two boys at

When part of a bone was exposed, it was soaked with shellac.

work under the direction of Mr. Peale. Two of them are half up to their waists in water. A huge wheel carries a series of buckets to keep down the water in the hole. Some of the workmen and onlookers wear tall beaver hats. It is a charming painting of life along the quiet Hudson River a hundred and fifty years ago.

The mastodon became the greatest attraction of Peale's Museum. But Mr. Peale died in 1827. Finally, in 1850 the exhibits of the museum were sold to P. T. Barnum's Philadelphia Museum. That was destroyed by fire the following year. Presumably the mastodon skeleton had burned with the other specimens. It was considered a great loss to science.

But in 1954, a letter came to Dr. Simpson of the American Museum of Natural History in New York from the Hesse State Museum in Darmstadt, Germany.

The German curator had no idea that Peale's mastodon had ever been lost or mourned. He said he wanted to remount the skeleton of Peale's mastodon. Would Dr. Simpson kindly send him photographs of another mastodon Rembrandt Peale had mounted? He understood it was in the American Museum.

Dr. Simpson was amazed. Eventually he determined

that the Hesse specimen was without doubt the long-lost Peale's mastodon. Then he got the history of its travels.

Some speculators had bought it from the Peale family before the rest of the exhibits were sold to Barnum. That was about 1847. So it wasn't in the Barnum Museum fire at all. It had been resold to King Louis Philippe of France. The King agreed to pay 100,000 francs for it upon delivery. He was going to put it in the Jardin des Plantes. But the mastodon got only as far as Bologne when the King abdicated and hurriedly left France. Somehow Peale's mastodon got to London. The British Museum didn't want to buy it, for they already had a mastodon.

The poor skeleton fell upon evil days. It was pushed around London for several years. Nobody wanted it. Finally, the Hesse State Museum bought it for a very small price. There it has been since 1854. Apparently it is in excellent condition.

The Warren mastodon was another skeleton discovered in the Hudson Highlands. It, too, became famous, but it was never lost. Right now it is one of the greatest treasures of the American Museum of Natural History in New York City.

All About Strange Beasts of the Past

It was found in 1845 on the Brewster Farm six miles from Newburgh, Orange County, New York. Like so many other prehistoric animals, it had sunk in a bog. When it was found, the skeleton was standing up. Six bushels of twigs lay where the stomach had been. Most of them measured about two inches in length. Some were as large as a man's finger; others were very small. Mixed with them was a mass of finely chewed leaves. Evidently that was the mastodon's last dinner. The bones, buried in a layer of pure shell marl, were perfectly preserved. They were light brown in color.

During 1845 and 1846 the skeleton was exhibited in New York and New England towns. At last Dr. John C. Warren, of Harvard University, purchased it for $5,000. It remained in Boston until 1906. Then Mr. J. Pierpont Morgan bought it for the American Museum of Natural History.

There the skeleton was carefully remounted under the direction of Professor Osborn. He wanted to be sure it was correct, so the man who did the work spent a whole day riding on the back of an elephant at the New York Zoological Park to study the way the bones lay. The skeleton is nine feet two inches high at the shoulder and nearly fifteen feet long. The long, low body is very broad, being six feet across the hips. This shows that the mastodon was quite different in shape from any kind of living elephant.

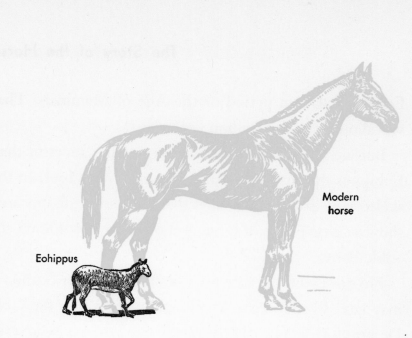

Modern
horse

Eohippus

8.
The Story of the Horse

Because you can see a horse almost any day, you may
not think of it as a strange beast of the past. But its great-,
great-, many times great-grandparents looked nothing
like the horse of today. Our modern horse has only one
toe and stands on its nail. But the first horse whose fossil
bones have been found had *four* toes on each forefoot
and *three* toes on each hind foot. He was a little animal,
barely larger than a cat. He has been named Eohippus, or
Dawn horse, because he lived in what is known as the

Eocene or Dawn period of the Age of Mammals. That was about fifty-five million years ago.

But we are sure there was an even earlier ancestor than Eohippus. It must have had five toes on each foot. In the skeleton of Eohippus the toes that had almost disappeared show as little pieces of bone in the proper position on the ankle bones.

No fossils of the five-toed horse have been found. It may have lived in Asia. We hoped to find it in the Gobi Desert of Mongolia. But strangely enough, we discovered no very early fossil horses. Perhaps they developed north of the Gobi.

Dawn horses have been found in England and Europe as well as in America. But there is no real evidence as to where they developed.

A dozen or more stages of early fossil horses have been found in the different periods of the Age of Mammals. Some lived in several parts of the world. However, the best-known series came from the western United States. There were several species of Eohippus. They varied in height from about ten to twenty inches at the shoulders.

Probably all of them were shy little beasts. They could run as fast as a dog, but the smaller ones must have lived in the forests. There, in the thick bushes and grass, they could hide from their enemies. They depended more upon concealment than speed. Of course we can't be sure, but possibly they were striped or spotted. Such coloration would have helped to protect them just as a tiger's stripes help conceal him in the jungle. The stripes blend with the stalks of grass and make the animal almost invisible. In the same way the spots on a baby deer look like light and dark shadows on leaves.

The ground in the forest where Eohippus lived was probably soft. Thus, his spreading toes gave him the best kind of support. They kept him from sinking into the moss and leaves.

The teeth of Eohippus were very different from those of living horses. They were short-crowned and showed that the animal ate leaves and other soft food. They were not at all like the high-crowned grinders of modern horses. Those are adapted for chewing dry, harsh grass.

During the fifteen or twenty million years of the Eocene or Dawn period, the early horses changed somewhat. Several different types developed.

Some remained about the same size, but some grew to be as large as a Great Dane. All traces of the fifth toes in the feet disappeared. At the end of the Eocene period, all the species still had four toes in the forefeet and three toes in the hind feet. Each ended in a separate tiny hoof. But the central toe of the forefoot had become definitely larger than the side toes. You can demonstrate for yourself why this was so.

Press your hand down on the table, with the fingers spread out. Now raise the palm of your hand until it is nearly vertical. Most of the weight of your hand rests on the tips of the three middle fingers. Your thumb and little finger do not even touch the table. They correspond to the two outer toes of the five-toed horse. Those toes disappeared gradually.

In running, the middle toe bore most of the animal's weight. It did most of the work. Because it was used so much, it grew bigger than the other two toes. But the side toes remained, for they were still useful.

By the time of the Oligocene period, about thirty-five million years ago, horses had lost the fourth toes on their forefeet. So they had only three toes on each foot. The middle toe was much larger than the side toes which just touched the ground. The best-known horse of this period was named Mesohippus. It was about the size of a wolf.

STORY OF

Millions of years ago the horse was no bigger than a house cat. Scientists have found its fossil bones with four toes on each forefoot. By studying the bones of many other fossil horses, they can tell how the horse has changed through the years.

Forefoot

Eohippus

Eohippus was a horse that lived about 55 million years ago. It had four toes on each forefoot and three toes on each hind foot. It was hardly bigger than a modern house cat.

Forefoot

Mesohippus

Mesohippus was the horse that lived about 35 million years ago. It had only three toes on each foot. The middle toe was much larger than the others. Mesohippus was about the size of a modern wolf.

THE HORSE

Merychippus

Forefoot

Merychippus lived in the Miocene Period, about 20 million years ago. It had three toes on each foot, but only the middle toe touched the ground. Some of the Miocene horses were as large as a modern pony.

Equus

Forefoot

Equus, the modern horse, has only one toe on each foot and stands on its nail. Tiny splint bones under the skin are the remains of the side toes its ancestors used to have.

All About Strange Beasts of the Past

A few million years later, another type had become as large as a sheep. Except for its feet, it must have looked very much like a tiny modern horse. The teeth were still adapted for eating soft vegetation, not hard grass. The brain had become much bigger and better. Horses were growing more and more intelligent.

The middle period in the Age of Mammals, the Miocene period, began about twenty-five million years ago. That was a time when the earth was changing. Mountains were pushed up from the lowlands. Regions that had been wet and warm became dry and cold. Forests were smaller, thinner and scattered. Open plains lay between them. Horses could no longer depend upon hiding in the thick vegetation for safety. They had to run away from their enemies so they developed speed.

The yielding, springy action of a three-toed foot was fine for soft and rough ground. But there was too much lost motion for speed on hard, smooth plains. For that kind of ground the firm step from a single, stiff toe was needed.

So, in the Miocene period, the horse's middle toe was much larger. It had a good-sized hoof which carried all the weight and did all the work. The side toes had become small and slender. They did not touch the ground and were seemingly useless to the horse.

Also, there were important changes in the proportions of the legs. They were longer in the lower parts and feet. Thus, the stride was longer, and the horse could run faster. He was a bigger animal. Some species were as large as many living ponies. His teeth had changed very much, too, so that they could grind hard grass. Thus, in feet and teeth and size, the horse had become adapted to life on the open plains.

In the Pliocene period, about ten million years ago, most horses still had three toes, but the side toes were very short. They were far above the ground.

One kind of Pliocene horse named Hipparion became a world traveler. He and others of his kind crossed from Alaska to Siberia over the land bridge. They spread all over Asia and Europe in vast numbers. Their fossils have been found all the way from China to western Europe. They must have lived in India, Spain and Greece and were probably the first horses to enter Africa. We found fossils of Hipparion in the Gobi Desert.

Another Pliocene horse had *only one toe on each foot.* Its name was Pliohippus. From its descendants came the one-toed horses of the genus *Equus*, which are living today. The evolution of a one-toed horse out of a three-toed horse is one of the most important events in horse history.

During the million years of the Pleistocene and Recent periods, horses have changed very little. In all species the side toes have almost entirely disappeared. Nothing of them remains except the splint bones under the skin.

Pleistocene horses were much bigger than their ancestors. The legs were longer and so was the neck. Also the skull was lengthened. The teeth had become completely adapted to eating coarse hard grass.

I have written chiefly about the feet of the horse because this feature is so easily seen and understood. But in the fifty-five million years of change from Eohippus to Equus, the whole body was altered. The teeth, the skull, the brain—every part was changed. The history of the horse is a wonderful example of evolution at work. It shows how an animal could adapt itself to a complete change of living conditions. Therefore, it continued to exist through fifty-five million years and up to the present time.

During the Ice Age, horses roamed in great herds over

the plains of North and South America and of Europe and Asia. Today, there are no wild horses in this hemisphere although they have survived in Europe and Asia. Why they disappeared from the New World, no one knows. It is one of the most mysterious happenings in animal history.

Scientists try to find some good explanation, but there really is none. Certainly, New World horses were not wiped out by the coming of glaciers in the Ice Age. Many horses lived where there were no glaciers. It couldn't have been lack of food, because there was plenty of grass for all the plains animals. There is not the slightest evidence that any new flesh-eater appeared to devour the horse. Moreover, the most dangerous carnivores, like saber-toothed tigers and dire-wolves, became extinct with the horses.

It has been suggested that some widespread disease killed all the horses. But if that is true, why did other plains animals like bison continue to live?

Wild horses were in America when the first people arrived fifteen or twenty thousand years ago. But there weren't enough men killing horses for food to affect their numbers.

Something, some great change of which we know nothing, occurred at the end of the Ice Age. The ground sloths, glyptodonts, mammoths, mastodons, saber-toothed tigers, and dire-wolves, all disappeared as did the wild horses of North and South America. Whatever the change was, these animals could not adapt themselves to it.

The fact remains that in 1519 A.D. there were no wild horses in North or South America. That was the date when the Spaniard, Hernando Cortes, arrived in Mexico. His soldiers brought with them sixteen horses and a colt born on the way. These were domesticated horses, of course. Through the years some domesticated horses escaped. They became wild and lived like their ancestors of the early Ice Age. A good many of these wild horses still exist in the western states. But they are not really wild horses. A wild animal is one whose ancestors have always been wild. These American "wild" horses are all descended from domesticated stock.

Even though wild horses became extinct in North and South America at the end of the Ice Age, they continued to live in Europe and Asia. The European ones were called *tarpans*. Some may still survive in parts of Russia.

Probably, however, they have mated with domestic horses.

In Africa the only wild members of the horse family living today are the wild ass, *Equus asinus*, and three species of zebra.

But in Central Asia there is a true wild horse. It lives in western Mongolia and Turkestan. The Mongols told me about this wild horse on my expedition into Central Asia. But we didn't go far enough west to find it. This horse has a jaw-breaking name—Przewalski's horse —after a famous Russian explorer. This is a small horse. It is yellowish-brown in color, with a dark mane and tail.

In the Gobi Desert, we did find another species of the horse family. It is called a wild ass, but it is not really a wild ass. Its scientific name is *Equus hemionus*. It lives in the driest part of the Gobi. Like many other desert animals, it seldom, if ever, drinks water. The starch in the vegetation it eats is converted into water in the stomach.

We were the first ones ever to photograph the Asiatic wild ass. It is a beautiful animal, about the size of a Mongol pony. The color is yellow-faun above, and pure white below. It has a wide, dark-brown stripe down the middle of the back.

In certain parts of the Gobi Desert, there are many wild asses. Sometimes we found them in great numbers. We had some exciting experiences photographing them. I wrote the story of one race with a big herd after I got back to my tent. This is the way it is described in my field journal:

"*White Lake, Gobi Desert, June 11, 1925.* Shackelford and I went out for motion pictures. The camera was strapped in the back of the car on its tripod. We stopped on the edge of a great basin, just behind the lake. We could see hundreds of yellowish forms shimmering in the desert heat waves. Wild asses without a doubt! Thousands of them. They were massed in three groups on the basin floor. For miles the horizon was dotted with stragglers.

"We circled far to the east, for the ground was soft in the basin. We wanted to drive them westward onto a gravel plain. There, for fifteen miles, it was fine going for the car.

"But a group of forty asses surprised us. They began to run rather slowly at first. Often they stopped to look at the car.

"As we drove on, dozens of asses came from miles

Hundreds of wild asses were pounding along on both sides.

away to join the first group. Hundreds were pounding along on both sides. The thundering mass kicked up such a cloud of yellow dust that we couldn't see or photograph.

"The whole galloping mass was not more than thirty yards away. Then Shackelford, with a whoop of joy, began 'shooting' with the camera. He ground off foot after foot of film.

"A few minutes later Shack shouted and pointed. A mare and her colt were coming in from the right. Out of the corner of my eye I saw a little wobbly, fuzzy thing.

All About Strange Beasts of the Past

It was doing its best to keep up with an anxious mother.

"I reduced speed and swung in beside the colt. The little fellow was not more than three days old. He ran in a stiff-legged, uncertain manner that was most amusing. He couldn't run fast, and he didn't seem frightened.

"We were right in the midst of the herd. Clouds of gravel spattered the windshield from the beating hoofs. Never have I had such a thrill! I'll remember it all my life!"

Now as I recount the story of the horse, I think of those hundreds of wild asses pounding beside us in the Gobi Desert. They remind me of their smaller ancestors, the wild horses of the Ice Age. Perhaps that is the way the early horses roamed over the plains of Europe, Asia and the Americas thousands of years ago.

Modern tree sloth

Ancient Giant ground sloth

9.

Some Very Strange Beasts

The Ground Sloth and His Relatives

One of our most peculiar animals today is the South American tree sloth. He seems particularly strange because he walks upside down hanging from branches. He even sleeps in this upside-down position.

The sloth is only about two feet in length. One species has three toes on each foot; another has only two. His head is small and round and his nose is blunt. His eyes and ears are little. He can't see well; neither can he hear very well. He depends upon his sense of smell and touch.

But at the end of his toes he has long, curved claws. These he hooks over a tree branch and moves along hand-over-hand on the *under side of the branch*. He spends his waking hours munching leaves and looking at the world from downside up instead of upside down.

We might call the South American tree sloth a "Strange Beast of the Present." And certainly his relatives that lived at the end of the Ice Age were "Strange Beasts of the Past." These relatives were the giant ground sloths that I wrote about in the first chapter. One of these was the kind of animal that the saber-toothed tiger tried to kill in the tar pit of La Brea. They were about as amazing as any animals we can imagine. The biggest was a mountain of flesh, perhaps twenty feet long and larger than an elephant. His scientific name is *Mylodon*.

He had great, curved claws on his feet, a thick, heavy tail, and powerful hind legs. In spite of his size and clumsy body, he was perfectly harmless. He only wanted to be left alone. His claws were for feeding, not fighting.

His favorite foods were leaves and the tender branches of trees. He would reach up, hook his claws over a branch, and pull it down. Then his long tongue, called "prehensile" because it was so well fitted for grasping, would shoot out and draw the leaves into his mouth.

Sometimes, by digging at the roots, he could tip over a big tree. A considerable number of skeletons of the ground sloth have been found with broken bones. Probably this was because many were killed by falling trees.

The ground sloth was covered with thick, coarse hair. It was brittle like that of the tree sloths that live today. In the under side of the skin of one kind of sloth, rounded chunks of bone were embedded. These made a sort of armor. Probably none of the big flesh-eating beasts of that time, except the saber-toothed tiger, could injure a full-grown ground sloth.

We know about this armor because of a remarkable discovery in a cave at Last Hope Inlet, Patagonia, South America. There evidence was found to show that ground sloths lived until a few centuries ago. Probably men had captured them. At least, the sloths were stabled or imprisoned in the cave.

Many bones and pieces of skin were dug up from a layer under the floor of the cave. This layer was composed of dust and ground-sloth manure. It was in a dry, protected corner of the cave. In the same place were man-made tools and weapons of stone and bone. Bundles of grass were spread as though intended for fodder.

The dry floor protected the bones and skin against dampness, and thus they were preserved. Some had bits of dried flesh and tendons clinging to them. Much of the hair was in perfect condition.

Until the discovery of this cave, it was supposed that ground sloths had died out many thousands of years ago. Now we know that they lived at least until men reached the tip of South America. I would give much to know how primitive men got the huge ground sloths into the cave. Perhaps they were driven into it by a group of hunters. Perhaps the animals used the cave as living quarters, as bears do.

If hunters found the sloths in their cave homes, they could have built a wall of rocks across the door of the cave. Then they might have thrown in bundles of grass or leaves to fatten the animals. Of course, they would have had to give them water, too. Eventually the sloths may have been killed like beef cattle.

All of these ideas are only thoughts of what *might* have happened. No one knows why those ground-sloth remains were in that cave, with the stone knives of primitive men. But they do prove that the giant ground sloth became extinct not so very long ago.

Many skeletons of ground sloths have been found, especially in Argentina. The animals evolved in South America when it was an island continent. Later, North and South America were connected as they are at present. Then the ground sloths spread northward. Their remains occur in various parts of the United States. Evidently sloths didn't do well here, for all of them died leaving no relatives.

The ground sloth was a member of the group of mammals known as the *edentates*. The name means "deprived of teeth." Such animals are without teeth or have no true teeth with enamel and roots. When teeth are present, they are like pegs and very simple. Of the edentates only tree sloths, anteaters and armadillos exist today.

Glyptodont

With the ground sloths lived another strange beast called the *glyptodont*. It was more or less related to the armadillo which lives today. The armadillo has a jointed "shell" made up of bony plates fastened together and covered with horny scales. Bands across the middle of the shell act somewhat like hinges so the creature can roll itself into a ball. Thus, it is somewhat protected from other animals that would like to eat it.

The huge glyptodont had a solid shell or carapace. It wasn't jointed, so the beast couldn't curl up as the armadillo does. It didn't need to, for no enemy could injure it. In addition, it had a bony cap on the top of its head. Also, the thick heavy tail was protected and had huge spikes at the end. It could be swung like a war club and was a terrible weapon.

Armadillos have claws on their toes for digging. But the short, round feet of the glyptodont ended in hooflike claws. Altogether, the beast looked much like a gigantic land tortoise and was often as much as fifteen feet long.

Glyptodonts wandered about the pampas quite unafraid. Their shells gave them complete protection. As they died, their huge shells would be left on the ground. One writer has suggested that primitive men might have used these shells as shelters in bad weather. It is possible, but we have no proof of this.

Glyptodonts lived at the same time and in the same places as the ground sloths. Like the ground sloths they

Ancient glyptodont

Modern armadillo

The ancient glyptodont had a solid shell which protected it.

migrated to North America during the Ice Age and later became extinct. Only fossils remain.

Irish Elk

While ground sloths and glyptodonts were living in America, one of the most magnificent of all mammals roamed in Ireland and northern Europe. It was the Irish elk, biggest of the deer tribe. But the name "elk" is misleading. It is not a true elk but an ancestor of the fallow deer—the small, spotted species often seen in European parks today. The Irish elk stood six feet high at the shoulders. Its enormous branching antlers spread eleven feet from tip to tip. Never was there a more royal creature.

Possibly the heavy antlers caused the death of these animals. Ireland has many peat bogs. The stags might have wandered into them while feeding on the tender green grass or drinking. If they began to sink in the treacherous swamp, they couldn't have leaped to safety because the antlers weighed too much.

Almost every peat bog in Ireland contains the skeletons of one or more Irish elk. The men find them when they dig out the peat to dry it for fuel. Usually the skeletons

The antlers of the Irish elk were the biggest of any deer that ever lived.

are almost perfect. But very few female elk are ever discovered. Probably because they had no antlers to weigh them down, the female deer could get out of the death trap.

The neck of the Irish elk was very strongly made.

That, of course, was to support the massive antlers. But the rest of the skeleton was graceful and delicate. The head was small for such a huge animal. The trim little feet and legs seem hardly strong enough to have carried such a big body.

What a wonderful thing it would have been to see an Irish elk alive! Its strength and beauty must have been breathtaking. Probably some Irishmen did see them, for they have been extinct for only a few centuries.

There is no good explanation for the enormous antlers of the Irish elk. Why did they grow so big? Certainly they were of little use to the beast except when fighting another elk!

Today we have a somewhat similar case in our modern moose. Their antlers are already so huge that they might someday destroy the creatures altogether. But probably man will kill them off long before their antlers do.

Titanothere

The word "titanothere" means a beast of titanic or enormous size. This strange beast has no other name. The titanothere was an amazing creature closely related to the horse and distantly related to the rhinoceros.

Nearly two hundred species have been named from their fossil bones.

The titanothere family began in the Eocene or Dawn period of the Age of Mammals. It flourished for perhaps twenty million years. Then it disappeared from the face of the earth.

While they lasted, the titanic beasts had a wonderful history. The earliest ones were not very big and were harmless. But in the last of their line, they reached their climax. That one was named *Brontotherium*, the Thunder Beast.

He was an enormous and terrifying creature. He looked a little like a rhinoceros. But he was much bigger, eight feet tall at the shoulder. On his nose he had a great, flattened horn divided at the top. It was a bony growth from the skull. The titanothere's skull, instead of curving upward back of its nose, curved downward like a soup dish. So the animal didn't have much room for brains.

Before my expedition went to Mongolia, titanotheres were only known to be from America. But Professor Osborn, one of the world's greatest paleontologists, had been studying them for a long time. Just as I was leaving for Central Asia, he said, "Keep your eyes open for

The skull of the battering-ram titanothere looks like a great western stock saddle.

titanotheres. I believe they came from Asia originally."

He was right. Almost at once we did find titanothere fossils. Many different kinds, too.

Of one of them Professor Osborn said, "It is the most distinctive and unusual fossil from Mongolia." The skull looks just like an enormous western stock saddle. The whole nose turns straight upward. It might be compared to the pommel of the saddle. No other beast has a head anything like it.

Professor Osborn believed that the animal used this great bony nose for "battering, attacking, tossing." He named the titanothere in my honor, *Embolotherium andrewsi*. The English translation would be "Andrews' battering ram-nosed beast." Apparently these titanotheres never got out of Asia, for their remains have been found nowhere else in the world.

Moropus

Of all the strange prehistoric beasts, Moropus is one of the most extraordinary. Scientists have never been able to decide why it was made the way it was.

It belongs to an extinct family known as the *Chalicotheres*. They are in the same group as the horses, tapirs, rhinoceroses and titanotheres. They have characteristics of all those animals, plus some peculiar ones of their own.

The neck and general shape of the head of Moropus remind one of the horse. The short, arched back, sloping hips and stubby tail suggest the tapir. The legs and feet are like those of a rhinoceros. The grinding teeth resemble a titanothere's. But the toes are the most remarkable feature. They are tipped with big claws. Of course horses, tapirs and rhinoceroses all have hoofs.

The first chalicothere bones were discovered in western Europe. Because of the teeth, scientists supposed that some of the bones belonged to an animal closely related to the titanotheres. The claws, they decided, probably came from a different animal, perhaps a giant *edentate* like a ground sloth.

But later a complete skeleton was found. The claws were attached to the toe bones, and the teeth to the same skeleton. Here was a beast unlike any other. Scientists tried to figure out why a hoofed animal like a horse should have claws. To this day there is no good explanation.

Chalicothere fossils have been found in Europe, Amer-

The Moropus resembled a horse, a tapir and a rhinoceros but had big claws on its toes.

ica and Mongolia. In the Gobi Desert we found a place where dozens of skulls and bones were packed in a solid layer. Perhaps some natural disaster had struck the animals down. But more probably the bones had been carried by a swift stream and dropped in a backwater or eddy.

All About Strange Beasts of the Past

Dinohyus

Dinohyus was another creature that seemed too strange to be real. It belonged to a group known as the *Entelodonts*, commonly called "giant pigs." Actually, they are not very piglike. They are not related any more closely to our modern pigs than to the cud-chewers, or ruminants.

Dinohyus was a very ugly animal, tall and solidly built. It had two-toed feet and a very big head with a long muzzle. Two tusks were large and strong. The tusks and

Dinohyus was an ugly big-headed creature.

all the front teeth were more like those of a flesh-eater than any vegetable feeder. But the back teeth resembled a pig's.

These great beasts must have been omnivorous—that is, they must have eaten both meat and vegetables just as bears, pigs and human beings do today. We found lots of *Entelodont* fossils in the Gobi Desert.

Other Strange Beasts

There were many other strange beasts which I can only mention. One was the giant kangaroo of Australia. It stood ten feet tall, had a head as large as that of a horse and a huge tail. Even with young in her belly pouch, the female could take twenty-foot leaps. It must have been a fantastic sight!

Also there was a camel that probably had no hump and grew a long neck like a giraffe. This was so it might pick off leaves from the tops of trees.

Another extraordinary creature was the Uintothere. He was a great lumbering animal with six "horns" on his head. These were bone growths and not true horns like those of a cow. Together with sharp, dagger-like upper tusks, they gave him a terrifying appearance. But really he was a stupid beast. His body got bigger from generation to generation. However, his brain did not. Maybe that was why he, and all his line, died at the end of the Dawn period, leaving no descendants even remotely related to them.

Thus far I have written only about the vegetable feeders, or herbivores. But there were many flesh-eaters, or carnivores, too. From the Dawn period all through the Age of Mammals, they killed and ate the others just as they do today.

The largest of all the carnivores was one I found in Mongolia, in the Valley of the Jewels. It was bigger than any other in the world, living or extinct, and was named *Andrewsarchus* in my honor. It was a huge wolflike beast, probably twelve feet six inches long without the tail. At the shoulder it must have measured six feet two inches high. *Andrewsarchus* lived in the Eocene period, forty-five or fifty million years ago. As yet, only that one specimen has ever been discovered.

The next most terrifying of the flesh-eaters was the saber-toothed cat, often called a saber-toothed tiger. I wrote about him in the first chapter. The saber-tooth was distinctly not a true tiger. His proportions were very dif-

Labels: Uintothere, Eohippus

Uintothere was a terrifying-looking beast with six so-called horns on its head.

ferent. His front legs were much longer and heavier than those of a tiger. The hind legs were shorter and weaker. This shows that the beast could not spring so far or so easily as a modern tiger. But once the great foreclaws were sunk in an animal they held it in a grip of death.

Saber-tooths spread to every continent except Australia. Those of North and South America grew bigger than any others. Why they died out all over the world during the Ice Age is a mystery.

10.
Beasts, Men and Caves

We know a great deal about the early mammals from their fossil remains. But we know more about the beasts of the Ice Age because people lived at the same time. They left us records of the animals in drawings, paintings, and sculpture found in the caves in Europe.

The most fearsome of all the flesh-eaters was the so-called saber-toothed tiger. No man ever saw a saber-tooth in America, for those ferocious cats were all gone before human beings arrived here. But in Europe our very early ancestors, called Neanderthal men, had to fight them. That was 30,000 to 100,000 years ago in the Ice Age.

The Neanderthal people were not handsome individuals. The women were only four feet three inches tall. The men averaged five feet four inches. They had thick bodies, short necks, long arms, and heavy legs slightly bent. Their heads were big with low, sloping foreheads. Bony arches overhung the eyes. They had small chins, but their jaws were heavy.

The Neanderthals were always hunters. At first they camped out on the plains. But year by year the climate became colder as the glaciers pushed down from the north. So Neanderthal men and women had to find shelter in caves.

But finding a suitable cave was not as simple as it sounds. Almost certainly the best caves would be occupied by cave bears. They were fearsome brutes as big as a large grizzly bear. If human beings wanted to take over the caves, they probably had to drive out the bears with smoke.

Frequently these early men kept wild animals away by building a rock wall across the entrance to the cave. Doubtless the bears would return night after night only to be driven off by a blazing fire in the mouth of the cavern.

Cave bears of that day looked much like the European brown bear of our time, but the head was larger and the legs shorter. They were abundant in Europe during the Ice Age. There must have been continual war between these cave bears and our early ancestors. In a single cave in France, more than 800 skeletons of bears were found.

In the Ice Age, cave men had to fight off ferocious bears.

One skull has a stone hatchet buried deep in the bone.

Bears and saber-toothed tigers were not the only animals our early ancestors had to drive away from their cave homes. Lions and hyenas were continually trying to get in, too. The lions, especially, were very dangerous for they were fierce and quick and strong.

Neanderthal people didn't leave us pictures of the Ice Age beasts, but people who came after them did. They are called Cro-Magnon men. They lived 15,000 to 30,000 years ago. Their art is the oldest we have yet discovered. These ancient people drew and painted pictures on the cave walls and even modeled animals in clay. Their pictures are so accurate that they have given us much information about the extinct Ice Age beasts.

Most of these caves are in the mountains of France and Spain. Several of the most important ones were discovered by children.

One cave was explored by the three young sons of the Count de Bégouen. A little stream runs into the mouth of the cave. The boys were always curious about where it went when it disappeared into the mountain. One day they got themselves a boat and rowed through the low cave entrance. The boat floated along a narrow passage

On the wall of an ancient cave in France, is this painting of
a woolly mammoth.

which opened suddenly into a gallery. When the boys
turned their lamps upward, they saw that the walls were
covered with drawings of extinct animals—mammoths,
woolly rhinoceroses, bison, and other beasts.

Of course, the boys were thrilled with their discovery.
It was the most exciting thing they had ever dreamed of
doing. So they continued to explore the cave. Finally,
they found a small opening in one wall. It was almost
hidden by fallen rocks. It looked interesting but dangerous. The boys just managed to squeeze through the hole.
It was the entrance into a low, narrow passage leading
upward.

All About Strange Beasts of the Past

Following it, the boys suddenly found themselves in a stately hall fifty feet long, thirty feet wide, and twelve feet high. Silent with awe, the young French boys flashed their torches around the room. At one end of the chamber lay a circle of stones. Near by, the sculptured figures of two great bison leaned against a mass of clay. A cow was in front, a bull behind. The clay was still soft. The moisture of the cave had preserved it so perfectly that thumb marks of the sculptor showed plainly. On the floor were prints of the artist's feet and the claws of cave bears. The cave was just as it had been when the men left thousands of years ago, never to return. Later the Bégouen boys found another great cave where the walls were covered with paintings of Ice Age beasts.

But they were not the only children who have made important discoveries of ancient animal pictures. In 1897 a Spanish nobleman, Marcallino de Sautuola, was digging for prehistoric stone tools at the entrance to a large cave in Spain. He had taken his small daughter with him. While her father worked, the girl wandered into the cave. In a great room at the left she looked up and saw wonderful paintings on the ceiling. Running back to her father she cried, *"Toros! Toros!"* meaning *bulls*. Grabbing his hand, she pulled him with her and pointed upward. Her amazed father saw a herd of bulls, deer, horses and other animals painted on the ceiling. Some were in black, others in red, and still others in both colors, beautifully shaded. They were so accurately done that even the species of the beasts can be determined.

An equally remarkable discovery was made in southern France by a fourteen-year-old boy named David. He became interested in cave exploration through a country priest.

On his father's estate, David found a hole in the ground

In the Cave of the Three Brothers, French boys discovered the figures of two great bison sculptured in clay.

near a grove of oak trees. "This," he thought, "might be the entrance to a cave. I'd better have a look." So in July, 1922, he wriggled through the hole into a passage. It led upward at a sharp angle into utter blackness. As David lighted a candle, the passage began to widen. Soon it opened onto a platform where the roof was much higher. He could see there was a bigger gallery farther on.

David didn't wait any longer. He ran back to his father who sent word to the priest. Together they explored the cave. At one time they nearly lost their lives. Poisonous gases filled a tunnel into which they had crawled. But finally they got through and emerged into a wonderous gallery. It is 400 feet long by thirty-six feet wide. The ceiling is twenty-three feet above the floor. And, wonder of wonders, forty paintings done in black and red decorate the walls. Mammoths, bison, horses and fish are represented. All the pictures are starred with mystic symbols.

Another young Frenchman named Castaret explored the Cavern of Montespan in France. It is a wonderful cave with vast halls and passages opening off a stream that runs through it. One of the halls is perfectly enormous. It is a majestic art gallery 750 feet long. The walls are decorated with paintings of bison, wild horses, mammoths, reindeer stags and hyenas. But most interesting of all are clay models of bears, horses and tigers.

One of the models is a headless bear, lying down. The body showed the marks of thirty spear thrusts. Fastened to the wall are three figures of tigers and another bear. All have jagged holes in them. Scientists believe that these holes were made by spears which men thrust into the clay models as though they were attacking them in real life. Probably the people of that day believed that an

This painting of bison was found in an ancient cave in Spain.

animal could be killed more easily if its image had been attacked with spears.

All of these relics tell us a great deal about early man and his way of life. His paintings and his sculpture tell us about many of the strange beasts that have since disappeared from the earth.

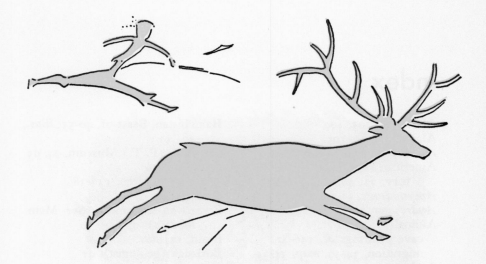

Index

Index

allabout
books